LOST IN TIME

Tony Pasqualini

BROADWAY PLAY PUBLISHING INC
New York
www.broadwayplaypub.com
info@broadwayplaypub.com

LOST IN TIME
© Copyright 2022 Tony Pasqualini

First edition: May 2022
I S B N: 978-0-88145-934-0

Book design: Marie Donovan
Page make-up: Adobe InDesign
Typeface: Palatino

LOST IN TIME was first presented by the Ensemble Studio Theatre of Los Angeles, at the Atwater Village Theatre, opening on 22 September 2018. The cast and creative contributors were:

DANNY PETRELLI .... Kevin Comartin
ROBERT ....Andy Shephard
GWEN WEST.. Tarah Pollock
AMY WEST.. Tonya Cornelisse

Director... Keith Szarabajka
Set design ....Amanda Knehans
Lighting design .... Brad Bentz
Costume design .... Robert Merkl
Sound design..Stephen George

CHARACTERS & SETTING

DANNY PETRELLI, 23, *grad student in sports journalism, time traveler*

ROBERT, 23, *grad student in accounting, DANNY's roommate*

GWEN WEST, 21, *acting student, DANNY's future wife, maybe*

AMY WEST, 24, *unemployed actor, GWEN's sister*

Place: Massachusetts, Vermont, Las Vegas, New York City, and Connecticut

Time: From September, 1974 thru June, 1975.

Simple, generic furniture pieces that can easily transform the stage from a student apartment to a theatre lobby, to a Vegas hotel room, to a Manhattan apartment, to a cemetery, to a porch.

For Sarah

ACT ONE

Scene 1

*(A shaft of light illuminates a young man, DANNY
PETRELLI, lying motionless in the middle of the floor. His
clothes are disheveled. He, suddenly, takes a sharp inhalation
of breath and partially sits up. He seems disoriented, hung
over. He stares around the room for a long moment, then…
slowly looks down at his chest, and puts his hand over his
heart.)*

DANNY: *(In quiet desperation)* Gwen…?

(We hear ROBERT's voice from the back of the stage.)

ROBERT: You up, finally?

*(Lights up on the rest of the stage—a spare, simple set
with generic furniture pieces: an easy chair parked in front
of a portable rabbit-eared TV, a small desk with a rotary
phone, a sofa, and downstage, two patio chairs and a bench.
ROBERT, DANNY's Boston University roommate stands
eating a bowl of cereal. ROBERT is wearing only a t-shirt
and boxer shorts. It's September, 1974. We are in the boys'
unkempt apartment in Brookline, Massachusetts.)*

ROBERT: I didn't realize you had that much to drink.
Must have passed out on the floor, huh?

(DANNY stares at ROBERT.)

DANNY: *(Deeply confused)* Ro…Robert?

ROBERT: *(Involved in his cereal)* I thought we both had early classes.

DANNY: How can you be here?

(Oblivious to DANNY's struggle, ROBERT takes a last bite of cereal, puts down the bowl and moves towards the front door.)

ROBERT: There's more cereal. A little stale though. *(Noticing his bare legs)* Oh, fuck! I don't have my pants on. Shit.

(ROBERT runs off to his room. DANNY pulls himself up off the floor. He looks around the apartment, not understanding what he's seeing.)

ROBERT: *(Offstage from his room)* I'm going to Allan's later if you want to come. Get a pizza.

(DANNY notices the desk with the rotary phone. He goes over to it and stares at it for a long moment.)

DANNY: The hell is this?

(ROBERT re-enters. He has his pants on and, as he walks, is trying to put on a pair of sneakers.)

ROBERT: You blowin' off your class? Fuck! I hate these sneakers.

(DANNY in the meantime has gone over to the rabbit-eared T V. Examines the rabbit ears)

DANNY: A joke. Must be a…

ROBERT: *(Still struggling with his footwear)* They like shrunk or something.

DANNY: *(Angry now) Robert!*

(ROBERT stops what he's doing.)

DANNY: *Why?* Why are you here?

ROBERT: *(Finally taking in* DANNY's *distress)* Because…
it's our apartment? You alright? *(Beat; no answer)* Okay,
I have a quiz this morning, I need to—

*(*DANNY *grabs him.)*

DANNY: *(Intensely)* Listen to me. Something is wrong.
Are you not aware of that?

ROBERT: With you?

DANNY: Yes, with me. With this apartment, with
everything.

ROBERT: Well, you're acting pretty weird, but
otherwise…

*(*DANNY *turns away from* ROBERT.*)*

ROBERT: Are you still drunk?

*(*DANNY *notices a mirror hanging on one of the walls. He
walks to the mirror. As he sees his refection, his knees buckle.
He touches his hair, his face, looks down at his waist. He gets
very close to the mirror now, staring hard at the reflection.*
ROBERT *is now intently watching him.)*

DANNY: *(Barely keeping it together)* Oh god. Oh god, oh
god, oh god oh god…. Help. Can somebody *help me!*
*(Pulls himself away from the mirror back into the room. He
is shaking.)*

ROBERT: *(No idea what to do)* Danny, what the hell…?

DANNY: The year?

*(*ROBERT *is too confused to answer.)*

DANNY: What is the year?

ROBERT: *(Scared)* It's…seventy-three. No, you got me all
confused, four, seventy-four. September, I don't know,
eighth or something.

DANNY: This is our apartment.

ROBERT: Yeah.

DANNY: In Boston.

ROBERT: In Boston, yeah.

DANNY: *(To himself)* Wake up. *(Beat)* Right now, wake up! *(Another beat)* WAKE THE FUCK UP!

ROBERT: Are you sick? Maybe I should I call your parents. Or that student health place…?

(DANNY ignores ROBERT. He reaches into his pocket and takes out a wallet. He finds a few dollars, and a driver's license, which he studies intently.)

DANNY: Oh fucking hell… *(He is trembling.)* Take a breath, will you. Just…I have to… This is not right.

ROBERT: Could be head trauma. You know, like you passed out drunk and hit your head on the coffee table.

(DANNY discovers a set of keys on a nearby table.)

DANNY: A car. I had a car. *(Turns to ROBERT)*

ROBERT: Ringo.

(DANNY doesn't understand.)

ROBERT: Your V W. Your Beetle.

DANNY: Where is it?

ROBERT: Where we parked. On Boylston. In front of the Pancake House, or, you know, half a block down.

(Holding the keys in his hand, DANNY slowly walks around the apartment.)

ROBERT: Goin' somewhere?

DANNY: *(Seems to be in a stupor)* Yeah. Maybe…I don't know yet.

ROBERT: You still have class, don't you?

DANNY: What class? I don't know anything about a class!

ROBERT: Check your schedule.

DANNY: *(Deciding)* Vermont. I'm going to Vermont.

(DANNY starts preparing to leave—tucks in his shirt, combs his hair, maybe finds a jacket.)

ROBERT: Oh. See the leaves?

DANNY: The what?

ROBERT: The leaves. Leaves turning? Autumn colors?

DANNY: Gwen...in Burlington, U V M. Seventy-four— you said seventy-four, didn't you?

ROBERT: Yeah, I...uh, yeah I did.

DANNY: Then she's there. She must be there.

ROBERT: Who's this now?

DANNY: I'm not dreaming, am I? Robert?

ROBERT: I don't think so. You're standing right here in front of me, and I don't think I'm dreaming.

DANNY: Okay...okay. I'll see you around then.

ROBERT: *(Completely baffled)* Okay. Have a good trip.

(DANNY turns and slowly walks downstage. As he does, ROBERT exits out the front door of the apartment.)

Scene 2

(The lights change. It is warm and beautifully bright. We are on the campus of the University of Vermont, in the lobby of the theater department. He looks around; not really knowing what to do next. After a few moments, GWEN WEST enters. She is twenty-one, attractive, an aspiring actress. She's a student here at U V M. She's dressed for hiking and carries a knapsack and a sleeping bag. She drops her knapsack. DANNY notices her.)

DANNY: *(Quietly)* Gwen?

GWEN: *(She has never seen him before.)* Uh, yeah. Hi.

DANNY: Gwen.

GWEN: Do I know you? Sorry if I've forgotten.

DANNY: You…? You don't, do you?

GWEN: I don't think so. We've met before?

DANNY: I…I guess we haven't, no.

GWEN: Maybe I have one of those familiar faces.

DANNY: You don't, absolutely not.

GWEN: But you know my name.

DANNY: I do.

GWEN: Were you looking at the photos?

DANNY: Photos?

GWEN: *(Pointing offstage)* Last year's production photos. *Romeo and Juliet*…the Nurse. Penny in *You Can't Take It With You*. *The Duchess of Malfi.* I'm prominently featured. *(Beat; prompting)* That's how you might know my name.

DANNY: *(Remembering)* You were the Duchess.

GWEN: Mm-hm. You didn't happen to see the production, did you?

DANNY: No. But, yes, I did see the photos.

GWEN: Very overwrought. Me, in particular. It's so hard to play middle age, you know what I mean. And yet every play… Of course, I'm not a conventional beauty. More of a character actor really. I probably won't get any professional work till I'm forty.

DANNY: I'm sure you were brilliant.

GWEN: Well…thank you, young sir. At last, a fan.

(DANNY and GWEN both smile.)

GWEN: So, what brings you to old Universitas Virdis Montis?

(DANNY *looks confused.*)

GWEN: It's what U V M stands for—University of the Green Mountains. We theatre students pride ourselves in mastery of Vermont trivia. *(Beat) Is* there a reason why you're here?

DANNY: *(No idea what to tell her)* Yes. Um…I'm here because…

GWEN: Are you applying to the department?

DANNY: Me? No, I'm… *(Latching onto this story.)* Actually, yes. I am applying. Sorry. Don't know why I'm so tongue-tied.

GWEN: Where do you go to school now?

DANNY: B U. Grad school…studying journalism.

GWEN: Cool. Sounds very romantic. Why would you leave that exciting world to idle your life away in the *theatuh*?

DANNY: *(Stumbling)* Um, don't know a hundred percent if I want to. But—

GWEN: School's already started though.

DANNY: I know, I—

(AMY, GWEN's *older sister, enters, looking quite disheveled. She is drinking from a cola can and singing*—Patty LaBelle's Lady Marmalade.)

AMY: 'Hey sister, go sister, soul sister--'

GWEN: Wow, right on time.

(AMY, *getting* GWEN *to dance with her:)*

AMY: "Gitchi, gitchi, ya ya, da da…" That drive is so boring! Lucky for us I got the tape player working… 'Gitchi, gitchi, ya ya here…'

GWEN: Stop already.

AMY: *(Notices* DANNY.*)*

Ooh, hello there. "Voulez-vous coucher avec moi?"

GWEN: Enough.

DANNY: Hi.

AMY: *(Couldn't be happier to see him)* Who the hell are you?

GWEN: This is my new friend, and fan. *(Grimaces)* Sorry, didn't get your name though.

DANNY: Danny. Danny Petrelli.

GWEN: Danny Petrelli, this is my sister, Amy.

(DANNY, caught off guard, stares at AMY.)

AMY: Soul sister, baby!

DANNY: She…? This is your *sister*?

GWEN: Is that surprising?

DANNY: *(Trying to cover)* Uh…it's not…no, I mean—

AMY: What's your story Danny Petrelli?

GWEN: He's thinking of transferring to U V M from B U.

AMY: Why the fuck would you want to do that. I mean you're living in Boston, go to N Y U if you want to transfer someplace. And besides if you're joining the theatre department, you'll have the walk in the shadow of Chip my-shit-doesn't-smell Armstrong. That's a burden no young thespian should have to bear.

GWEN: All right, we don't need the critique.

AMY: *(Talking to DANNY)* No, but, really, I *love* Chip. How can you not love someone who is a certified expert on everything?

GWEN: *What* is the matter with you?

(AMY snuggles up in one of the chairs.)

AMY: All this fresh air gives me a headache. All I want to do is sit here and drink. Can't I stay here and drink with your new friend Danny, and you go to Smuggler's Snatch by yourself.

GWEN: Notch, Smuggler's Notch. You have rum in that coke?

AMY: *(A southern belle)* Of course not, silly. How ever could you imagine such a thing?

GWEN: Give it to me. *(She takes the cola can and sips; it's strong.)* Oh, Jesus. You'll be on your ass if you drink this.

AMY: That's the idea, genius.

*(*GWEN *holds out the can to* DANNY.*)*

GWEN: Here, this will prep you for life in Burlington.

DANNY: Better not.

AMY: You guys are both pussies. Particularly her. *(To* DANNY*)* But you knew that already, didn't you?

GWEN: Shall we get going?

AMY: Starving. Need food.

GWEN: The cafeteria's open. *(To* DANNY*)* We reserved a campsite in Smuggler's Notch for the weekend. Ever been?

DANNY: Never heard of it.

AMY: What? You never heard of Smuggler's Snatch? Why it's one of the great tourist attractions of the world.

GWEN: Shut up. It is a little in the backwoods, but very pretty. We are going to hike, build campfires, eat s'mores...

AMY: Then shoot ourselves out of boredom. Why don't you tag along, Danny. Chippy is staying on campus so he can chase all the hot freshman girls—

GWEN: Working on his directing thesis. *(To* DANNY*)*
He's reimagining *The Oresteia* as American soldiers
returning from Vietnam.

AMY: Because a theatre nerd from Montana knows so
much about that.

GWEN: Research. Ever hear of it?

AMY: Anyway, Danny here looks like he could use
some fun.

GWEN: I'm sure Danny has other things to do this
weekend besides getting drunk with you.

AMY: I wasn't thinking of him for me.

GWEN: *(Embarrassed)* Okay, that's enough now. Go to
the cafeteria, I will be there in a minute.

*(*AMY *stands up.)*

AMY: Give me five dollars.

GWEN: You didn't bring any money? Really?

AMY: I brought the car. Come on, don't be such a
cheapskate.

*(*GWEN *digs into her bag and pulls out a five.)*

GWEN: Here. I'm trying to save up for our Christmas
trip, you know.

AMY: Right, you and Chip off on a wonderful skiing
adventure. In a wonderful ski lodge, with wonderful
hot chocolate. Far out, man. *(To* DANNY*)* Have lunch
with us at least, Danny boy. She's ripe for the picking.

GWEN: *(Firmly getting rid of her)* Go.

*(*AMY *grabs the cola can from* GWEN.*)*

AMY: Mm, methinks the lady doth protest too much.
Bye then, you love birds.

GWEN: *Go! God.*

DANNY: Goodbye.

(AMY *is gone.* DANNY *doesn't look well.*)

GWEN: How does one put up with that? That's what I'd like to know.

DANNY: *(More to himself)* That's Amy. Good Christ.

GWEN: My point exactly. *(Beat)* You *can* have lunch with us if you like.

DANNY: Well…

GWEN: Or we can find Dick Cobb. He's head of our program. He'll be able fill you in on all the grisly details.

DANNY: *(Sitting)* Maybe…I'll just sit here for a minute if that's okay.

GWEN: Sure. Any questions for me? About U V M.

DANNY: No, I, uh…can't seem to think of any.

GWEN: Are you alright?

DANNY: Yeah…I'm…I'm alright.

(GWEN *watches him for a moment, not sure whether to leave or stay.*)

GWEN: You watch the resignation?

DANNY: *(No idea)* The…?

GWEN: Nixon?

DANNY: Oh. Right, yes…that happened. Of course, yes, I watched.

GWEN: Goodbye, Tricky Dick, don't let the door hit you on the way out.

DANNY: Mm-hm.

GWEN: Kinda sad, too. I almost felt sorry for him.

DANNY: Don't. He had it coming.

(GWEN *watches* DANNY…*deeply now, almost as if she's reading his mind.*)

GWEN: You *sure* you're alright?

DANNY: A little woozy, maybe.

GWEN: No one's around, you could take a nap.

DANNY: No.

(Beat)

GWEN: Probably should get going…

(GWEN reaches for her knapsack.)

DANNY: This morning I woke up in my apartment. I lived near BU, in Brookline. Did I tell you that before? Well, I did. Uh, *do.*

GWEN: Got it. You live in Brookline.

DANNY: Yes, and what's unusual about that is…last night I went to sleep in California.

GWEN: Really?

DANNY: *(He nods.)* San Francisco. *(Takes a moment here, then…)* In my wife's and my house.

GWEN: You're married.

DANNY: Yes.

GWEN: A little young.

(DANNY has no response.)

GWEN: Were you kidnapped from California? Drugged and whisked away on a plane?

DANNY: No, no, I wasn't. You see, my wife…well, she *has been* my wife for quite a long time.

GWEN: Okay. Like an arranged marriage, when you were eight or something?

DANNY: Oh, god no. Uh…no. We were married…well, we've been married for…thirty-five years.

(Beat. GWEN sizes up the situation.)

GWEN: This is a joke, right? Like a prank? Maybe Amy set this up, although it seems a little sophisticated for her drink-addled brain. Someone else from school maybe?

(DANNY *stands now and starts to pace.*)

DANNY: That's what I thought at first. A very elaborate prank. On me, not you. But how does that explain the fact that earlier today I was standing in my grad school apartment, everything the same as I remember, except...I haven't lived in Boston for over forty years. And look at me...I'm no longer this sixty-four-year-old. I'm this kid, with hair, for god's sake, and not a penny to my name. How do you explain all that?

GWEN: I would have no way of explaining it.

DANNY: Right. Of course you wouldn't.

GWEN: I would still ask, though...

DANNY: Yes?

GWEN: Why would you come all the way to Vermont?

DANNY: Maybe this is enough for now.

GWEN: And be waiting here by yourself outside our theatre department?

DANNY: *(Struggling)* Okay, let me ask you this first. Does anything I've said, or my presence here, resonate in any way that you might think I'm not completely insane?

GWEN: Not sure what you're asking.

DANNY: In the deepest recesses of your mind, in some faint subconscious memory, perhaps...do you recognize me at all? Gwen. Gwenny. Gwendolyn Mary West. *(Beat)* Do you?

(GWEN *stares at* DANNY, *not knowing what to say. Then...*)

GWEN: Wow. What are they smoking down there at B U? (*No answer. She picks up her knapsack.*) See ya, Danny Petrelli.

(GWEN *walks offstage. As she leaves…*)

Scene 3

(ROBERT *enters. He is finishing a joint. He sits on the sofa. He appears deep in thought. A Crosby, Stills, Nash and Young record is playing in the background. We are back in* DANNY *and* ROBERT's *apartment. The next day*)

ROBERT: (*His mind pretty well blown*) Whoa.

(ROBERT *takes a toke, holds it up to* DANNY, *who shakes his head.*)

ROBERT: You told her all that?

DANNY: I did.

ROBERT: And you're transferring to U V M?

DANNY: No, that was an excuse. Only one I could think of.

ROBERT: What did she do?

DANNY: Took off. She was pretty freaked out.

ROBERT: Yeah, no shit.

DANNY: I knew it was wrong to tell her, even to go see her in the first place, but I was desperate. I thought maybe she'd be having the same experience. Now she must think I'm some kind of lunatic.

(*Beat;* ROBERT *is struggling with this information.*)

ROBERT: Huh. So…okay, wait…you *did* make all this shit up, right?

DANNY: No. Why would…you think I made up this story, then went to see a random girl in Vermont and told her the whole thing?

ROBERT: I don't know, man.

DANNY: I'd have to be insane.

ROBERT: Yeah, except—

DANNY: I mean is that what you think?

ROBERT: Did you call your parents?

DANNY: Yes, I called. *(Almost laughing)* They're alive, kicking around. We had the same annoying conversation we always used to have…

ROBERT: *(Getting ahold of himself)* Sure…no, but…yeah, okay…yeah, but…but wait a minute…

DANNY: Yes?

ROBERT: I can't… Okay, this is what I'm trying to fully comprehend… You were like *old*, like you lived a whole bunch of your life and then yesterday morning, *presto*, you're back here now.

DANNY: That's what I believe happened, yes.

ROBERT: The *same* you.

DANNY: Yes, the same me.

ROBERT: *(Deeply considering)* Huh. Okay…huh. *(Beat. Then he nods.)* Cool beans.

DANNY: You believe me?

ROBERT: Of course, man, a hundred percent.

DANNY: Are you sure? Because I don't even know if I believe myself.

ROBERT: *An Experiment with Time*, J W Dunne.

DANNY: A…what? Who?

ROBERT: I told you about this, didn't I? Before he died, my Uncle Edgar was really into this guy—this British guy from like fifty years ago, who wrote a book about his dreams predicting the future.

DANNY: I'm not predicting anything; I experienced the future. I was just there in the future.

ROBERT: Right, exactly. See J W Dunne's theory states that all past, present and future time isn't linear, but all kind of bunched up together, kinda like in string theory. And it's just our limited perception that makes us see the order of the moments we happen to see them in. In reality, though, he's saying all the moments are right there for the taking, we just don't know how to access them, except sometimes accidently in our dreams.

DANNY: I'm not dreaming, Robert, that much I'm sure about.

ROBERT: I know, that's why this is so amazing. You must have this, I don't know, kind of advanced consciousness. And here's what proves it—you're different, deeper somehow, a different person. I knew it but couldn't figure out what it was. Now it all makes sense. You've seen your future, just like J W Dunne wrote about. This is *fucking* cool!

DANNY: Hold on—

ROBERT: *(On a roll)* And when you have this higher consciousness, you like have all these millions of moments, then you choose when to live.

DANNY: I *choose*?

ROBERT: Yeah.

DANNY: Why would I choose right now?

ROBERT: Oh, well, because…yeah, I don't know, man.

DANNY: It makes no sense. I have to go through this whole part of my life again? Finishing grad school, which I hate...that horrible summer job at the Ledger. I have to live in *Newark* again! My job at the Chronicle doesn't happen for another five years. I'm not even supposed to meet Gwen for another two. I mean, what's the point?

ROBERT: What does she do during this time?

DANNY: After school moves to New York, pursues her career... We meet in San Francisco. She happens to be staying in my apartment building for a memorial service, and—

ROBERT: Whose?

(DANNY *takes a moment.*)

DANNY: Doesn't matter. I forget. Anyway, we talk one night, end up going for a walk, having a drink... afterwards, we can't stop seeing each other.

ROBERT: Then you guys live happily ever after. That's righteous, man.

(DANNY *shakes his head.*)

DANNY: No.

ROBERT: But you said she was your wife.

DANNY: She is. Has been for a long time. Except we didn't live happily ever after. Especially not in the last...christ, ten years.

ROBERT: Like my parents, I hate that shit.

DANNY: Yeah, no kidding. (*A realization begins*) Wait a minute.

ROBERT: Yeah?

DANNY: (*Figuring this out*) Is it possible...? If I'm here now, it can only mean I'm getting a second chance, right?

ROBERT: Uhhhhh, yeah. Right.

DANNY: *(Understanding)* And if I'm getting a second chance, nothing has to be the same, does it?

ROBERT: No. Or, I mean…what do you mean?

DANNY: Let's say this J W Dunne theory is true— experiment with time, I *choose* when to live. I *choose* now. Nothing random about it.

ROBERT: Uh-huh.

DANNY: Which means, starting now I redo my life, my entire life, change whatever I want. So, if I want, Gwen and I can start our relationship tomorrow, later this afternoon, anytime at all. Fuck Newark.

ROBERT: Sure, except…yeah, maybe we get that J W Dunne book out of the library, first. Check on a few of the concepts. Might be best to meet when you're originally supposed to meet, you know, adhere to the prime directive.

DANNY: This isn't a *Star Trek* episode, Robert.

ROBERT: I'm just saying the prime directive might be applicable in this case.

DANNY: It's not. And even if it were, Gwen and I have already met. If I wait the two years and meet her in San Francisco she'll remember me as that weird guy from Vermont.

ROBERT: I should call my aunt.

DANNY: No, Jesus, don't call anybody.

ROBERT: But maybe she can help. Uncle Edgar used to talk all the time about—

DANNY: It doesn't matter, no one else can know. We keep it between ourselves. *(Making a plan.)*

Gwen always loved my letters; it was a thing between us. I'll write her a letter, apologize. Make up a reason why I told her all the time traveling stuff. Then, slowly, we start our relationship, or as soon as possible. Hell, it'll be so much better—all the years we spent together I was blundering around in the dark. I can understand now, see things more clearly. *(Feeling a surge of optimism)* I can change our lives. I'm getting a second chance, Robert. It's a *fucking miracle!*

ROBERT: Absolutely, man.

(Pause. DANNY and ROBERT are alone with their thoughts.)

ROBERT: What about us?

DANNY: Us?

ROBERT: I mean we stay friends, right?

(DANNY hesitates.)

DANNY: Uh, sure, yeah, of course.

ROBERT: In San Francisco.

DANNY: Right, San Francisco.

ROBERT: And we really hang out and do shit together? Like our kids play together while the wives are out shopping. We watch the Red Sox, smoke dope, shit like that?

DANNY: You have it all planned out, don't you?

ROBERT: Fuck, yes. Do we?

(A moment)

DANNY: Giants not the Red Sox.

ROBERT: Damn. Okay, but for real?

DANNY: Yeah. Yeah, wouldn't have it any other way.

ROBERT: Cool, man. *(Looks at his watch.)* Argh, shit! Gotta calculus test in five minutes. *(He hurries towards the door.)*

DANNY: You just smoked a joint.

ROBERT: Much better that way. *(Stops suddenly)* Danny, quick—what's my future wife's name?

DANNY: *(Stumped, then…)* Scarlett Johansson.

ROBERT: Oh, that's sick. Is she beautiful?

DANNY: Yeah, now get out of here.

ROBERT: *(Gleefully)* Fuck you, man! *(He hurries out.)*

Scene 4

(Lights change—still in the Boston apartment, but it is now late evening, about a month later. DANNY idly walks around the apartment mostly looking at the closed bathroom door. Finally, he flips on the T V. From the T V, we hear a David Frost interview with Mohammed Ali, a month before the Foreman-Ali fight—The Rumble in the Jungle. He watches the interview intently. After a while, GWEN enters from the bathroom. She's wearing a man's bathrobe.)

GWEN: When was the last time you washed this bathrobe?

DANNY: I don't think I've ever washed it.

GWEN: Nice.

DANNY: I actually didn't know you could wash a bathrobe.

GWEN: What, you just thought you wore them till they corroded from the stink?

(GWEN curls up in the easy chair. DANNY shuts off the T V.)

DANNY: *(Deciding to sit next to GWEN)* Move over.

GWEN: No.

DANNY: You're really not going to let me sit next to you?

GWEN: No.

DANNY: Should we talk?

GWEN: I wanted to talk before. That's why I'm here in Brookline, if you recall.

DANNY: Did I stop you?

GWEN: You kissed me.

DANNY: Not unrequested.

GWEN: Bullshit.

DANNY: I asked if you wanted to get a bite to eat, to which you replied… "I can eat in Vermont, you spaz. What are you standing there for?"

GWEN: Okay, so what?

DANNY: So…you said, 'what are you standing there for' and I responded. Which is what you seemed to want.

GWEN: Amy brought a bottle of tequila in the car. I was not fully in control of myself—

DANNY: How was I supposed to—

GWEN: —you should have known.

DANNY: —figure that out?

GWEN: Doesn't matter.

DANNY: Not like I threw you down on the sofa and ripped off your clothes.

GWEN:Might as well have.

(DANNY *gets a chair and brings it close to the easy chair.*)

DANNY: Look, really, I'm sorry—

GWEN: I don't know why I'm here. No idea. This is not the kind of person I am.

DANNY: What kind of person is that?

GWEN: Who lies to her boyfriend. Cheats on her boyfriend. Chip thinks I went with Amy to see an improv show.

DANNY: You wanted to come.

GWEN: I wanted to *talk* to you. Because I was confused. Because all that stuff you sent me...

DANNY: *Stuff*...?

GWEN: Your letters.

DANNY: I was expressing to you how I feel. You couldn't have been that confused, you kept writing me back.

GWEN: Yes, and I don't know why the fuck I did that either. What's happening here between us, Danny, is *not real.*

DANNY: No? Because from my perspective I don't think it could get much more real.

GWEN: We don't know each other, though. And now... what you're doing right now...

DANNY: What am I doing?

GWEN: This whole attitude you have...I have this horrible feeling you're trying to brainwash me, and here I am falling for it.

DANNY: Jesus, *wait*, wait a minute. I would never... never in a million years would I ever do anything like that to anyone.

GWEN: Then what is it with you? How could you possibly have these feelings for me? *(He starts to talk.)* And please don't start again about returning from the future.

DANNY: I apologized for all that. I never should have said any of that stuff.

GWEN: It makes you sound crazy.

DANNY: I know, I know it does. But I'm not, I promise.

GWEN: Then explain to me exactly where this infatuation comes from?

DANNY: It's what I tried to tell you in my letters...those pictures of you in the drama department—

GWEN: On the basis of three or four crummy production shots no one could possibly—

DANNY: No, not just on that basis, but, yes, when I saw those pictures I felt...I *knew* you were the person I was going to spend the rest of my life with. Right then. Yes, that's what happened. And then when you were standing in front of me five minutes later, I...I was overwhelmed. That's why I blurted out all that crazy stuff because...I was overwhelmed by the feelings I was having. And, you know, based on our recent contact, based on the events of this *very night*, based on your own actions, I wasn't exactly wrong, was I?

(GWEN *takes a long time here, struggling with the question.*)

DANNY: Was I?

GWEN: *(Looking away)* Not exactly wrong, no.

DANNY: Then what's the problem? *(No answer)* Chip?

GWEN: Duh.

DANNY: He's irrelevant.

GWEN: Not to me.

DANNY: To *us*. He's irrelevant to us, to our future.

GWEN: He's my boyfriend. He's been my boyfriend for two years. Let's put things in the proper perspective, shall we.

DANNY: I suppose it won't help to tell you, we'll be together a lot longer than you and Chip ever—

GWEN: No, it fucking well won't. *(Beat)* Amy will be back in a minute. I should get dressed.

DANNY: You could stay the night. I'll drive you up to Burlington in the morning—

GWEN: No.

DANNY: Chip is expecting you?

GWEN: He is, as a matter of fact.

(GWEN *is getting dressed. Trying to show as little skin as possible, yet not leaving the room.* DANNY *approaches her.*)

DANNY: Okay…what if we try again next weekend? We'll go slow this time. Talk more before…

GWEN: I'm starting rehearsal. And could you please not stare at me.

DANNY: Kinda hard not to.

(GWEN *gathers up the rest of her clothes.*)

GWEN: I'll change in the bathroom then.

(DANNY *very gently holds*GWEN.)

DANNY: You're beautiful, you know.

GWEN: Hands off.

DANNY: Everything about you. You're this amazing human being—

GWEN: And you're a fucking liar. Are you going to let me go?

DANNY: *(Reluctantly)* Yes, okay, I'm letting you go.

(DANNY *takes his hands away;* GWEN *is staring at him.*)

DANNY: Uh…do you *not* want me to--?

(GWEN *kisses* DANNY, *quite passionately.*)

DANNY: *(When he has a chance)* So, no letting go, right?

GWEN: Shut up.

(DANY *and* GWEN *continue to kiss; clutching at each other as they stumble onto the sofa. Suddenly, she pulls away.*)

GWEN: Enough. That's enough. God, what is the matter with me!

DANNY: *Really*? Because—

GWEN: Don't talk.

DANNY: Getting seriously mixed signals here.

GWEN: I mean it. *Do not talk.*

(After a lengthy pause)

DANNY: What are you rehearsing for?

GWEN: *(Frustrated with herself and him)* You see, this is my problem right here.

DANNY: No, honestly, I just want to know what you're starting rehearsal for.

GWEN: Why do you care? *(He shrugs.)* Fucking Our Town, all right?

DANNY: The great American play, *Our Town*?

GWEN: Yes.

DANNY: That sounds like fun.

GWEN: I thought it would be. It was supposed to be.

DANNY: Until…?

GWEN: Dick Cobb once again screwed me over.

DANNY: How did he do that?

GWEN: I've always, *always* wanted to play Emily, but, oh no, he had to give it to sweet little Susie Plum, who I'm sure will be *so* wonderful in the soda fountain scene but will totally butcher the final act which is the actual point of the whole fucking play.

DANNY: Well, don't hold back on your feelings.

GWEN: Not funny.

DANNY: *(A vague memory)* Wait… Susie *Plum*?

GWEN: Yes. Do you know her?

DANNY: *(Can't place her)* Uh, not sure… Anyway, who are you playing?

GWEN: Mrs Gibbs. Which is a fine role when you're *forty-five.*

DANNY: And Chip?

GWEN: What about him?

DANNY: Is he in the cast? *(She looks away.)* He's the love interest.

GWEN: No shit, Sherlock.

DANNY: Yeah, I can see how that would suck. *(Remembering now)* Oh…huh.

GWEN: Not like he has a thing for Susie Plum. I mean I'm not worried about him running off with her, but still having to sit around and watch those fucking scenes. It's going to be so annoying.

(DANNY moves away from GWEN.)

DANNY: Yeah, well, you never know, maybe something good will come of it.

GWEN: Like what? What good could possibly come of it?

(DANNY shrugs, rather suspiciously.)

GWEN: Do you think you know something?

DANNY: No. Know something about what?

GWEN: About Susie and Chip.

DANNY: Why would *I* know anything?

GWEN: I don't know, why would you?

DANNY: Uh, I didn't say a thing.

GWEN: No, but you're *implying* an awful lot.

DANNY: Well, you're *reading* an awful lot into a few very innocuous statements.

GWEN: Am I?

DANNY: Yes, you're the one trying to convince herself that Chippy isn't going to get all hot for sweet Susie Plum.

GWEN: My god…you are, aren't you? Fuck you. You are deliberately trying to make me paranoid.

DANNY: What? You brought it up. I don't know these people. I'm just picking up on your vibe.

GWEN: Yes, and instead of reassuring me like a decent person would do, you want to take advantage of the situation, because wouldn't it be so convenient for you if Chip went ahead and dumped me for that stupid little twat.

(DANNY *wants badly to answer but decides against it.*)

GWEN: What? Now you have nothing to say?

DANNY: I don't know what you want me to say.

GWEN: I want you to tell me what is actually going on in that head of yours, because I am sick of playing these games.

DANNY: Okay, what's going on in my head, Gwen, is that, obviously, Chip is going to fall for Susie, because that's what assholes do, and you are, in case you haven't noticed, dating a *colossal asshole*!

(*Right at this moment* AMY *and a very stoned* ROBERT *enter the apartment.*)

AMY: We're back. What's happening? What did we miss? I see some naughty children without a lot of clothes on.

ROBERT: I bet they're playing hide the salami.

AMY: Is that what you two naughty children are doing, playing hide the salami?

GWEN: *(Quietly; focused only on* DANNY*)* You know I came here to find out about you—why I was feeling the way I was feeling. Honestly, I had no idea what I might find.

DANNY: Gwen—

GWEN: But thank you…because you just made it all very clear for me. *(Turns to* AMY*)* I'm getting dressed. Then we're leaving.

AMY: Okeydokey.

ROBERT: Okeydokey, Smokey.

DANNY: For god's sake, Gwen—

GWEN: No. Stop interfering with my life, okay? Please don't call, and please don't write to me anymore.

*(*GWEN *picks up the rest of her clothes, goes to the bathroom and slams the door.)*

DANNY: Argh! *Fuck!*

*(*AMY *glides into the room.)*

AMY: Apparently, that didn't go as planned.

DANNY: What do you care?

AMY: I care a lot, believe it or not.

ROBERT: *(Giggling)* That's a rhyme.

AMY: It was intentional…and maybe somewhat unprofessional.

ROBERT: *(Enjoying himself)* Then you better go to a confessional.

DANNY: Guys, shut up.

AMY: Sorry. *(Beat; then quietly)* We were being totally reprehensible.

*(*AMY *and* ROBERT *are laughing uncontrollably.)*

DANNY: Where'd you get so high anyway?

ROBERT: Allan's house. They're having a party.

AMY: You have cute friends, Danny.

DANNY: Cute?

AMY: Well, complete dorks, yet charming in their own idiotically-syncratic ways.

DANNY: Sorry we don't meet your *high* standards.

AMY: Okay, pal, you may not be aware of this but I'm your biggest supporter.

ROBERT: Not as big as me, hussy.

AMY: I stand corrected.

ROBERT: That's better. No young wench is usurping my place. Huzzah! *(He flops down on the floor.)*

DANNY: Why would you be my supporter?

AMY: Because Chip happens to be one of the great jackasses of all time. If I have to spend one more Thanksgiving listening to him expound on his theories of the *theatuh,* I'll be forced to stab him in his rather effeminate mouth with a carving knife. Therefore, I'm very open to Gwenny-girl dating an Amazing Kreskin wannabe.

DANNY: *(Confused)* Amazing Kreskin?

AMY: You heard me.

(DANNY takes a moment to understand.)

DANNY: *(Looks hard at ROBERT)* Oh, shit, Robert. Did you...? Dammit. I told you not to go blabbing that around.

ROBERT: I'm sorry, but—

AMY: I was persistent

ROBERT: She was persistent. She wanted to know all about you.

DANNY: What *exactly* did you tell her?

ROBERT: Not what you think. Just that you have…like visions of the future.

(ROBERT *tries to covertly wink at* DANNY.)

DANNY: Visions of the future.

ROBERT: Yeah. And, hey, she's cool with it.

AMY: No.

ROBERT: You told me—

AMY: I told you he's bullshitting you.

ROBERT: And I told you, there are more things, Horatio, in heaven and earth.

AMY: *(To* DANNY*)* And you are, aren't you? Bullshitting.

(AMY *waits for an answer;* DANNY *just stares at her.*)

AMY: *Aren't* you?

DANNY: I'm not bullshitting anyone.

AMY: Prove it.

DANNY: I can't.

(*Pause;* AMY *watches* DANNY.)

AMY: All right then, tell me something you see in the future.

ROBERT: He sees all, he knows all.

AMY: Do you see Gwen moving to Montana with Chip, after they graduate?

DANNY: That doesn't happen.

AMY: No? Because young Chippy is heading west to start the next great American theatre, all the while convincing Gwen to join him in the fun.

DANNY: She doesn't move to Montana.

ROBERT: This is the man who would know.

AMY: I'd say it's almost a done deal.

DANNY: She moves to New York. She wants to live in New York.

ROBERT: *(Singing)* "New York, New York, it's a helluva town, the Bronx is up and the Battery's down—"

DANNY: The thing with Chip doesn't work out.

ROBERT: That's right, the future is inevitable, let it happen baby.

AMY: Yet, strangely enough, they cancelled their ski vacation and are now taking an exciting Christmas jaunt to you-know-where.

DANNY: *(Caught off guard)* What?

AMY: Gwen and the Chiclet got themselves plane tickets. He's showing her around that urban mecca of Bozeman, Montana. Is that part of your inevitable future?

ROBERT: *(Worried)* Bummer. Is it?

DANNY: *(Angry)* Gwen's relationship with Chip doesn't work out! I don't know anything about Montana. It's difficult for me, at the moment, because I have nothing…no money, no job prospects…I have another year of school then after that—

AMY: It'll be too late.

DANNY: Why would you say that?

AMY: Because she's too fucking gullible, too easily talked into Chip's bullshit. If you know her as well as you claim to, you'd know that was true. So, if I were you, Kreskin, I'd lose the clairvoyancing, and take some fucking action.

(Pause. DANNY stares at the T V.)

ROBERT: *(In deep thought. A la Strother Martin)* What we got here is failure to communicate.

DANNY: *(Makes a decision)* Fuck it, you want action?

ROBERT: Bitchin', baby.

DANNY: I'll need money up front first, but then...

AMY: What?

DANNY: Easy—rent an apartment in New York, transfer to N Y U, ask Gwen to move in with me.

AMY: Just like that.

DANNY: Why not? Better than living in Bozeman, Montana.

ROBERT: Where would *I* sleep?

AMY: How would you get this money?

DANNY: *(Smiles)* Ali-Foreman.

ROBERT: Foreman's going to kill Ali, man. Lower the BOOM!

(DANNY is quiet.)

ROBERT: He's not?

DANNY: *(To* AMY*)* You have money, right? Trust fund.

AMY: I'm buying a co-op.

DANNY: Wait a couple of months, buy a bigger one.

*(*AMY *sizes* DANNY *up.)*

AMY: How big?

DANNY: Depends how much you come up with—thirty K, Forty? Forty would be better. Odds are four to one at least. If we bet the round, we'll clean up.

AMY: You're serious.

*(*DANNY *shrugs.)*

AMY: Where would we place this bet?

DANNY: Vegas. We'd have to go to Vegas.

AMY: You and me, go to Vegas.

ROBERT: Cool, man, put ten dollars down for me.

DANNY: Wouldn't have to be both of us.

AMY: Fuck that. When exactly does this great excursion occur, Kreskin?

DANNY: The fight's postponed, back on in a month or so. We go the day before.

(AMY *is staring at* DANNY.)

ROBERT: *(Celebrating)* I'm gonna make forty dollars, man!

(GWEN *enters from the bathroom and heads to the front door.*)

GWEN: Let's go. *Now.*

(GWEN *is quickly out the door.* AMY *stands and slowly follows* GWEN. *When she arrives at the door, she turns back to* DANNY...)

AMY: Tell me the truth, Danny boy...you really see the future?

DANNY: Only one way to find out.

(AMY *smiles, does a bit of an Ali shuffle.*)

AMY: 'Float like a butterfly...sting like a bee.'

(AMY *exits.* ROBERT *pulls himself off the floor; he is quite woozy.*)

ROBERT: Gotta go to bed, Allan's shit messed me up.

DANNY: Okay.

ROBERT: Hey...think I have a chance with Amy?

DANNY: No.

ROBERT: Really?

DANNY: Trust me, you don't want to get involved.

ROBERT: Fuck. Fuck me. I never live happily ever after. Do I ever?

DANNY: Sure, you do. Give it time, brother.

ROBERT: *Ah*, Scarlett what's-her-name, right?

DANNY: Yeah. Get some sleep, man.

(ROBERT *starts off.*)

ROBERT: Night, John-Boy. *(He re-enters.)* Wormholes.

DANNY: What?

ROBERT: Another theory I been thinkin' about.
Einstein's relativity—warped space-time can be
connected by wormholes.

DANNY: And…?

ROBERT: Like in the future, if you entered a wormhole,
you might have come out the other end in the past.

DANNY: Yeah, I don't remember entering a wormhole,
though.

ROBERT: Okay. Just a thought.

(ROBERT *starts off…then stops.*)

ROBERT: Multi-verses? (DANNY *stares at him.*)

(ROBERT *weaves offstage.*)

Scene 5

(DANNY *quickly puts on shoes, a dress shirt and sport
jacket. Lights change. We are now a month or so later,
in a room at the Flamingo Hotel, Las Vegas. He turns a
radio on and continues getting dressed. From the radio we
hear the post-fight broadcast from the Ali-Foreman fight.
During this,* AMY *enters from the bathroom. She's wearing
a startlingly sexy dress. She carries an open bottle of
champagne.*)

AMY: Whoa-hooo! We are winners, baby. Ali, Ali,
Aliiiiii!

DANNY: *(Clicking off the radio)* You better believe it. The sweetest boxer in the history of the sweet science.

AMY: I have *never* felt this good in my entire fucking life. To visions of the future! *(She takes a big drink.)*

DANNY: *(Toasting with a soda)* Visions of the future.

AMY: *(Notices DANNY's change of wardrobe)* Ooooh, don't you dress up nice.

DANNY: Thanks. Not so bad yourself.

AMY: *(Modeling)* What I am wearing this evening, Mr Petricelli—

DANNY: Petrelli.

AMY: Whatever…is an authentic Diane von Furstenberg. A little splurge of mine.

DANNY: All for me?

AMY: No, Bozo. For myself. I had planned to unveil this beauty on Christmas Eve, midnight mass, give all those staunch Episcopalians a treat. What do you think Mommy will say?

DANNY: Take it off, you disgusting slut?

(AMY roars with laughter.)

AMY: Yes, yes, exactly. And what do you say? No bullshit. What do you really say?

DANNY: *(Conceding)* I say…you look pretty hot.

AMY: You bet your ass, Danny Petroleum. How much did we win?

DANNY: A lot. We won a lot.

AMY: So, what next?

DANNY: Next?

AMY: Yeah, what do we bet on next? Roulette, blackjack…

DANNY: We stand pat. Enjoy a nice dinner, maybe a late show, then get the hell out of Dodge.

AMY: *Boooring*. I want to gamble, baby. We are on a winning streak. We got to strike when the iron is hot, hot, hot.

(AMY *is dancing around the room.*)

DANNY: Hey…*hey*. We are not on a winning streak. I have no intention of blowing this money on anything besides the aforementioned dinner.

AMY: *(Teasing)* Aforementioned, oooh, I use big words.

DANNY: And I would suggest you do the same. You're not a gambler.

AMY: I am. I'm a big gambler in case you haven't noticed.

DANNY: Do you even know how to play blackjack?

AMY: I gambled forty thousand dollars on you, Petrewhatever. And for your dining and dancing pleasure I *do* know how to play blackjack. First one to eighteen wins. There, asshole.

DANNY: Twenty-one.

AMY: Prig.

DANNY: Nevertheless, I'm sure you'll be grateful for my sagacity in the morning.

AMY: "Sagacity"…*really*? That's the word you're going to fucking pull on me.

DANNY: It means—

AMY: I know what it means, dickwad. You sound like my father.

DANNY: Well, I obviously have no way of preventing you from gambling away your—

AMY: No, you certainly *do not*.

DANNY: —winnings, but I would strongly suggest you consider—

AMY: YES, I get it. Christ! I'm having some fun with you. Can't a girl have fun?

DANNY: Sure, you can have fun. Have all the fun you want.

AMY: You bet your ass I will! *(Beat; she stares at his ass.)* Maybe a little prurient fun. You know what *that* means, Mr Dictionary?

DANNY: Uh, yeah, I do.

(DANNY turns away from AMY.)

AMY: Awww, worried what Gwenny will say? She'll never know.

DANNY: Whether she does or not is hardly the point.

AMY: God, what an old fart you are. You don't think she's bonking Chip right now as we speak.

DANNY: I really don't know and—

AMY: You should hear them when he visits at home. They spend hours going at it. In her childhood bedroom no less— "Ooooh....ooooh...Chip, Chip, Chip"

DANNY: That's enough, Christ. What is the matter with you?

AMY: Don't you know? You know everything else. Or you say you do.

(DANNY shrugs.)

AMY: What *do* you know, Dan? I'm supposed to be your loving sister-in-law, right? What visions do you have about *my* future? Nothing. Do you pay no attention to me whatsoever? *(She smiles at him.)* Come on, Danny. You never envision this? *(She starts to remove her top.)* Huh? Tits on a clamshell.

(DANNY, again, turns away.)

AMY: God, what a pussy. *(She holds out the bottle.)* Champagne, at least?

DANNY: I don't drink.

AMY: *(Amazed)* What the fuck is next with you?

DANNY: I don't drink *anymore.*

AMY: Oh, *anymore.*

DANNY: I spoiled something. I don't want to do it again, all right.

AMY: I spoil shit all the time.

DANNY: Yeah, well, it's a bad habit.

AMY: Guess you and I have that in common. You know, stud, you may be chasing the wrong sister.

DANNY: *This* does not happen between us. Get it through your head!

AMY: I'm doing you a solid, pal.

DANNY: What kind of *solid* exactly?

AMY: To disillusion you of your illusions.

(DANNY looks confused.)

AMY: Christ, what a dope. You really believe all this ends with you and Gwen locked together in eternal matrimonial bliss?

DANNY: Well, yes.

AMY: *(Laughing)* Unbelievable. You're meant to be *gap* boyfriend. The bridge between Chip and whoever she's finally ending up with. That's all you were ever meant to be.

DANNY: According to you.

AMY: Yes, according to me.

DANNY: What happens in my relationship with your sister is none of your damn business. You lent me money to bet the fight, I appreciate that. But this is it. This is where our paths diverge. I'm not a *gap* boyfriend. That maybe was your idea, or scheme, but it was never mine. Gwen and I have our whole lives ahead of us, which you are not a part of.

AMY: *(Stung)* I'm not? Really?

(DANNY doesn't answer.)

AMY: I have no part at all to play in your wonderful future fantasy life?

DANNY: I...of course you do, I only meant...

AMY: You may not realize this, Dan, but a girl like me needs to have a little fun once in a while, fucking *needs* a little fun, otherwise...otherwise she gets too sad, too lonely. Otherwise, she has bad thoughts. So, I'm sorry if I offend you. And disparaged your 'great love'. Not that it fucking matters anymore. Ha-ha-ha.

DANNY: What does that mean?

AMY: Your 'gap' is officially closed, pal. You lost out to Chip. If you want any more West pussy, you'll have to settle for me, the deranged sister.

DANNY: I told you—

AMY: Gwen's agreed to move to Montana. Blah, blah, blah, blaaaaaah.

DANNY: Never! That *never* happens.

AMY: Au contraire. There was a big blow up a few weeks ago. Apparently, Chippy was sniffing around some hot little actress. Gwen, infuriated anyone would deign to betray her, broke up with him; and the Chiclet, realizing he was losing his meal ticket came sniveling back, and voila! They're in love again. When

they go to Bozeman next month, they'll be looking for
a place to live.

DANNY: *(Shocked)* She took him *back*? Why the fuck
would she take him back?

AMY: Like I told you—vulnerable to bullshit.

DANNY: *(Trying to understand)* But how could…?
(Quietly to himself.) Shit—because I warned her, she
knew in advance; because she knew in advance, she
acted differently.

AMY: Don't give yourself so much credit, Sigmund.

DANNY: I need to talk to Gwen. *(He goes to the room
phone.)*

AMY: I've already tried talking. Pretty fucking
hopeless. Also, it's two in the morning in Vermont.

(DANNY puts the phone down. Paces around the room.)

DANNY: As soon as I get back, I'll look for the
apartment.

AMY: Sure, that'll work.

DANNY: What is the matter with you? Are you
purposely trying to screw me up here?

AMY: Don't shoot the messenger. Besides, I am offering
a sweet consolation prize.

(AMY moves towards DANNY.)

DANNY: God, have some…

AMY: What, self-respect? I'm pathetic cause I ask for
what I want? Cause I'm not *pretending* I'm someone I'm
not.

DANNY: How am I pretending?

AMY: This undying affection for Gwen. "Oooh she's
my future wife, I'll love her forever, we're soul mates."

DANNY: You really don't know what you're talking about.

AMY: *(Like a cat with a mouse)* Fuck me and you'll find out.

DANNY: You're crazy.

AMY: You'll find out exactly what I'm talking about.

DANNY: I need to see Gwen.

AMY: Yeah, well, it ain't happening tonight. *(She's close to him now.)* Come on, Petrelli, it ain't rocket science. Be a fucking man. And I'll be a "fucking" woman.

(DANNY grabs AMY.)

AMY: *(Surprised, at first)* Hey. *(Beat; then softer.)* Hey.

(AMY and DANNY are on the verge of a kiss, but he pulls away.)

DANNY: *(Flustered)* No, no. I told you, this does not happen. I'm going for a walk. *(He pulls some money out and throws it down.)* Get yourself something to eat.

AMY: I have my own money, stud.

DANNY: I can't help you, Amy. I really can't. I'm sorry.

(DANNY quickly leaves the hotel room.)

AMY: *(Calling after him)* Who the fuck asked for your help! *(Beat; then to herself)* Story of my life.

(Lights fade)

END OF ACT ONE

ACT TWO

Scene 1

(Lights up. We are now in DANNY's *New York apartment—almost two months later. The front door is slightly ajar.* ROBERT *is onstage. He has four books by J W Dunne—author of* An Experiment with Time. *He is reading one of the books and will, occasionally, write something in a notebook. After a few moments, we hear a knock.)*

ROBERT: *(Looks up from his work)* Enter.

*(*GWEN, *in winter attire, opens the front door.)*

GWEN: Robert?

ROBERT: Oh, hey, yeah, Gwen. Danny told me you were coming. Come on in.

GWEN: Not disturbing you, am I?

ROBERT: No, no, doin' a little research here, that's all. Come inside, look around. Snowing, huh?

GWEN: It is. *(She takes off her wet coat.)*

ROBERT: Danny went to get bagels…wasn't sure what time you were getting in.

GWEN: *(Looking around the apartment)* Wow. This is quite a place.

ROBERT: I know, right.

GWEN: Two bedrooms, I'm impressed.

ROBERT: Danny was hopin' you'd like it.

GWEN: Was he?

ROBERT: Uh-huh.

GWEN: And you're living here now.

ROBERT: I'm supposed to go back to Boston after New Year's, finish school, but I gotta secret plan.

GWEN: Do you?

ROBERT: Hope it works.

GWEN: Me, too. *(Pointing at his books)* What are you researching?

ROBERT: This is…uh, well my uncle was into this guy, J W Dunne. I checked these books out of the library.

GWEN: *(Looking through them)* Serial Universe, An Experiment with Time, Nothing Dies…interesting.

ROBERT: Oh yeah, it's, uh, a whole new way—well not so new, guy wrote this stuff fifty years ago – a *different* way of looking at life, and, well, *time*. How we perceive time.

GWEN: How do we?

ROBERT: Uh…as a matter of fact, just got to this interesting part. Turns out, or according to Dunne's theory, there are these different levels, well, an eternity of levels of time. Like we're in *time 1*, you and me right now, livin' our lives, but then when we die, we're transcended to *time 2* and from there we can look down on all the time we spent in *time 1* and, you know, revisit it all or whatever part of it we want to…revisit.

GWEN: *(Not convinced)* Okay…?

ROBERT: And the proof is, when we dream, we sometimes dream about the future, right? Things that haven't happened yet. And only in our dream world can we—

GWEN: Wait, wait, wait…we dream about the future?

ROBERT: Yeah, not always, but yeah, sometimes…cause the barriers that limit us are down and we can observe things from *time 2*. In our dreams. I don't know, does that make any sense? If you write down your dreams first thing in the morning you can prove it to yourself. I been doing that now for a couple of months.

GWEN: Does it work?

ROBERT: Definitely. That airplane crash in Virginia a few weeks ago…? Night before, I dreamt about it. Not exactly, you know, but similar. Oh, and a couple of years ago, right before the draft lottery came out, my uncle called me, I mean literally from his deathbed, and said… "you're getting a high number, guaranteed, somewhere in the two-nineties".

GWEN: And…?

ROBERT: Two-ninety-seven. Pretty amazing, right? Kept me out of the Mekong Delta.

GWEN: I'll have to try this out.

ROBERT: Keep a notepad by your bed.

(A beat. She smiles at ROBERT.)

GWEN: Does Danny read these books?

ROBERT: Uh…no, not…no. I've told him a little bit about them.

GWEN: I see.

ROBERT: *(Trying to cover)* Yeah, I don't think he necessarily believes…or…I don't know what he thinks of the whole idea actually.

GWEN: It would explain a lot though, wouldn't it?

ROBERT: How's that?

(DANNY enters with a large bag of fresh bagels, and two cups of coffee. He sees GWEN.)

DANNY: Hey, you're here already.

GWEN: I am.

DANNY: Sorry to keep you waiting. I have bagels and coffee. Can you believe this weather?

GWEN: I love it. I've had breakfast, though.

DANNY: Been here long? (*He takes off his coat. Then sets out the bagels*)

GWEN: A few minutes.

ROBERT: I been explaining to her about old J W.

(ROBERT *points at the books.* DANNY *sees what he is referring to.*)

DANNY: (*Concerned*) Oh. That's...uh, that's funny, isn't it? A little obsession Robert has.

GWEN: Mm-hm.

ROBERT: (*Suddenly excited.*) Shit, Danny I forgot to tell you, I have good news. This morning I talked to this guy at Columbia—you know, about my situation—I think everything's gonna work out. Need to get my father to sign off but—

DANNY: (*Flustered*) Robert... Let's not deal with this right now, okay. I'd like to show Gwen around.

ROBERT: Oh yeah, absolutely, got some more reading anyway. Can I...? (*Refers to the bagels*)

DANNY: Go ahead.

ROBERT: Thanks.

(ROBERT *takes three bagels, and a container of cream cheese. He takes a big bite of a bagel. He then gathers his books and notepad.*)

ROBERT: (*With his mouth full*) I love pumpernickel. Nice to see you, Gwen. Saw Amy the other day.

GWEN: Yes, she told me.

ROBERT: She gave us decorating ideas.

GWEN: Uh-huh.

ROBERT: This place could use a woman's touch, you know what I mean?

DANNY: Robert...

ROBERT: Oh, okay. Bye-bye. *(With his arms full, he goes into his room, and, clumsily, shuts the door.)*

DANNY: He's back to Boston in a couple of days.

GWEN: Doesn't sound like it.

DANNY: Well, he is. *(Beat)* I'm glad you came.

GWEN: Can't stay very long.

DANNY: No?

GWEN: My parents are having a party tonight; I agreed to help. I wasn't around for Christmas so I'm feeling obliged.

DANNY: I see.

GWEN: How about you?

DANNY: What?

GWEN: Were you home for Christmas?

DANNY: No, stayed here. Wanted to fix the place up.

GWEN: Your parents must have been disappointed.

DANNY: Ah, not so much—called hourly, swallowed poison, threw themselves on a burning pyre. Italian families.

GWEN: Could be worse. I don't believe my parents noticed I was missing.

DANNY: I know that's not true.

GWEN: Do you?

DANNY: *(Hesitates)* Bagel? Coffee?

GWEN: I'm fine, thanks. *(Looks around.)* It's a great apartment, Danny. Everyone I know wants to live in the village, but no one can afford it.

DANNY: I'm lucky.

GWEN: I'd say so.

DANNY: I mean I got a good deal on the place. And, please, if I ever suggest getting rid of it, hit me hard with a baseball bat.

GWEN: I will. If I happen to be nearby.

(Beat)

DANNY: I'm glad you came.

GWEN: You said that already.

DANNY: Ah, sorry. Why *did* you?

GWEN: You asked me.

DANNY: Yes, but…

GWEN: And I was worried.

DANNY: About…?

GWEN: You and Amy. Your trip to Las Vegas.

DANNY: What about it?

GWEN: Betting all that money on the fight. Knowing exactly how it would turn out.

DANNY: I…I'm majoring in sports journalism, you know, so…it's an area of expertise. I researched the fight, looked at it objectively, not emotionally…

GWEN: But you knew what round the fight would end.

DANNY: Educated guess. Lucky guess. Definitely luck involved.

GWEN: Amy says you have visions of the future.

DANNY: That's…that's Robert's idea. It's—

GWEN: But when we first met you told me—

DANNY: And then later I told you I had made all that stuff up. Which I had. I...I have no visions of the future, all right? Just very...distinct feelings. Nothing magical going on here.

GWEN: And what about Amy?

DANNY: What about her?

(GWEN *looks at* DANNY.)

DANNY: You think I'm taking advantage of her?

GWEN: Do you know why she didn't graduate from college?

DANNY: I... (*Thinks about this for a moment*) No, I really know nothing about her school years.

GWEN: She was at Oberlin. Second semester, middle of winter. She was found on the roof of her dorm— screaming, drunk, naked. God knows what was in her head, or what might have happened.

DANNY: Yes...okay, I see.

GWEN: I don't want her hurt. She can't be hurt.

DANNY: Well, we're...there's nothing going on between us, if that's what you're thinking.

GWEN: No?

DANNY: No. I mean...I convinced her to bet the fight, but I swear I would have paid her back if we lost.

GWEN: I'm not just talking about the fight.

DANNY: There's nothing else. She came over to see the apartment.

GWEN: She's had a couple of awful relationships—real jerks, who *did* take advantage of her. "Borrowed" money from her. She's drawn to people like that.

DANNY: That's not me. That's not what is going on between us. She made quite a bit of money back from that fight as a matter of fact, so—

GWEN: I want to make sure you know exactly what the situation is, because—

DANNY: I do.

GWEN: —she could have killed herself that night Danny. She may have wanted to. I don't even really know. But you cannot lead her on—

DANNY: I'm not leading her—

GWEN: —into believing that you have feelings for her. When you *don't*.

DANNY: I swear to you, I am not doing that.

(Long pause, then GWEN *speaks quietly.)*

GWEN: She can't be hurt again.

DANNY: Okay.

GWEN: Okay. *(Beat)* I'm going home now.

DANNY: You haven't even been here ten minutes—

GWEN: *(Curtly)* Sorry.

*(*GWEN *gets her coat and moves towards the door.)*

DANNY: Wait. Can you…just wait another…a few more minutes. I—

GWEN: What for?

DANNY: There's something I want to discuss with you. Since you're here now, this would maybe be a good time.

GWEN: My parents are expecting me back—

DANNY: I know. I know they are, but this is important. I think when I tell you, you'll understand how important this is.

GWEN: I'm worried about Amy. I didn't come here for any other reason.

DANNY: Sure, I get that, nevertheless you are here, and…I have a proposal for you.

GWEN: Oh god, Danny—

DANNY: No, hear me out, please. Please.

(GWEN *stares at him for a moment. Sighs)*

GWEN: Fine, go ahead.

DANNY: I have two bedrooms. I did that intentionally.

GWEN: For Robert.

DANNY: No, not for Robert. I told you, Robert… he won't be living in New York. But here's what I thought…

GWEN: *(Worried about what's coming)* Really, Danny—

DANNY: It's for you. The second bedroom. I realize I completely jumped the gun with our relationship. I went way overboard. We need time to get to know one another. And I *know* after you graduate you want to live in New York. You just said you love the village. Well, here we are. Here's your place. I'll finish school, you can pursue your career and we'll…we'll get to know one another. More than we do now—

GWEN: You're asking me to be your *roommate?*

DANNY: Okay…it's an unusual arrangement, all things considered, but…we'll see how things go between us. Give it a chance. Enjoy the city, enjoy the beginnings of our lives…enjoy each other, and…see how things go. No pressure.

GWEN: Seems like it would be nothing but pressure.

DANNY: It won't, I promise you. It's a great time to be in New York. You're a terrific actress, I'm a pretty good writer, we'll…we'll have an amazing life. We'll be a team, you know. Help each other. Support each other. Completely different from the last time. A whole new beginning.

GWEN: What last time?

DANNY: No, I just meant…I mean, I'll be different, I'll…I won't force you to live somewhere you don't want to live.

GWEN: I'm moving to Montana.

DANNY: Yes, I heard about that—

GWEN: Bozeman. Where Chip's from.

DANNY: This is exactly what I'm talking about. You can't possibly choose to live in Bozeman-fucking-Montana—

GWEN: It's a beautiful—

DANNY: —when I'm offering you-

GWEN: —place and—

DANNY: —your dream apartment—

GWEN: Listen to me! Chip has these amazing ideas about running a theatre, which I think could really work—

DANNY: But you want to live in New York—

GWEN: —and which I want to fucking participate in.

DANNY: Bullshit.

GWEN: Bullshit yourself.

(Phone rings.)

DANNY: Give it some thought. That's all I'm asking. Then in a few weeks I'll come up to Vermont and we can—

GWEN: No. Do *not* come up to Vermont.

DANNY: We'll meet somewhere else then. Wherever you want—

(Phone rings.)

GWEN: Danny, I'm not having this discussion with you anymore.

DANNY: *Anymore?* We've *never* had this discussion.

GWEN: We don't have a future together. I don't know how else—

(Phone rings again.)

GWEN: —I can explain it to you.

ROBERT: *(Shouting from offstage)* Telephone.

DANNY: *(Shouting back)* Let it ring. *(To GWEN.)* You're wrong about that.

GWEN: If you come up to Vermont, if we meet again, nothing will be different—

(Phone rings. ROBERT enters.)

ROBERT: Sure you don't want me to get it?

DANNY: Fine, take it into your room though.

ROBERT: Hey, I was thinking, on Friday Allan can get his brother's truck, maybe I can move in my stuff —

(As the phone rings again…)

DANNY: *(Snapping at him)* Robert, *not now!* Just get the phone, will you.

ROBERT: Yeah, okay. Geez.

(ROBERT takes the entire phone and pulls it onto his room, closing the door behind him. The phone rings once more before he answers.)

GWEN: If we could be friends, then maybe—

DANNY: Oh, for *Christ's sake*! This is not about us being *friends*. You feel the same way I feel. We're meant to be together—

GWEN: Chip and I are getting married. So, no, we are *not* meant to be together. That is not—

DANNY: *(Panicked) Wait.* You say…? You're getting *married*?

GWEN: In June. After we graduate.

DANNY: *(Trying to control himself)* Listen to me. You do not marry this fucking guy. You do not throw your life away on someone you don't even really love, when the person you *do* actually love – a person who will return that love back to you faithfully for the rest of your life—is standing right here—

GWEN: I'm leaving now.

(DANNY is blocking her way.)

DANNY: —in front of you!

(ROBERT enters again. He looks very distressed.)

GWEN: Get out of my way.

DANNY: *(At his breaking point)* This is not supposed to happen!

GWEN: Do you want me to scream, because I will.

ROBERT: Danny…

DANNY: I want you to look at me, really look, and tell me you have no feelings for me.

GWEN: I'm getting married. That's all you need to know—

ROBERT: Danny, you gotta—

DANNY: *(Viciously turning on him)* Robert, can you not see we're having a conversation here.

ROBERT: Yeah, but your mother's on the phone. She really needs to—

DANNY: Take a fucking message, I will call her back.

ROBERT: Yeah, but—

DANNY: I'll call her back, Robert!

GWEN: Go talk to your mother, I'm leaving.

DANNY: You don't understand.

GWEN: I understand everything. And yes, I do have feelings for you. Obviously. This whole thing has been torturing me for months. This apartment…this is my dream apartment we're standing in. I'd like nothing better than to move into your second bedroom, or hell even your first bedroom. But I can't. I'm not. I'm marrying Chip. I decided, I promised, and that's the end of it. (*She walks past him towards the door.*)

DANNY: (*Blurting this out*) We have two kids. Two kids together. A boy and a girl.

GWEN: (*Shocked*) What…? What are you saying?

DANNY: They're older now. Twenty-five and twenty-nine, but they're great. I mean, they had problems like all kids do, a lot they had to work through, but they're both in great shape—

ROBERT: You really need to talk to your mother.

GWEN: How do you know that? You're just making this up.

DANNY: I'm not. I know it. I've experienced it. We've experienced it together.

GWEN: You told me—

DANNY: (*Rattling this off*) Yes, I told you the truth to begin with, and then I *lied* because I was afraid I had scared you off. But this is the truth now. It's all insane I know, but we live our lives together, you and me. You don't marry this guy—

ROBERT: *(Getting desperate)* Danny!

DANNY: —I'm sure he's a perfectly nice but he's not who you're meant to be with.

GWEN: *(She's truly scared now)* There's something wrong with you. You...you need help. Psychological help.

ROBERT: You need to talk to your mother now, Danny.

DANNY: *(Losing it) Robert, Jesus, I just told you—*

ROBERT: Your father's dead.

(Everyone stops—stunned by the news.)

ROBERT: That's what she's calling about. He had a heart attack this morning. She found him outside...been shoveling snow, I guess. She called an ambulance, but too late.

DANNY: My father doesn't...he doesn't die for...that can't be right. He's still alive. They must have saved him because—

ROBERT: That's what she told me.

DANNY: He doesn't die now. Not for another...I don't know...fifteen years at least.

(A beat)

DANNY: HE DOESN'T DIE NOW.

ROBERT: *(Quietly)* You better talk to her.

(DANNY, in a state of shock, turns downstage. GWEN slowly exits. ROBERT meanwhile gets a tie and overcoat for DANNY. He helps him put the tie on and then the coat. ROBERT then exits.)

Scene 2

(DANNY *walks downstage and sits on a bench. It is about a week later, late morning. We are in a New Haven cemetery, right after his father's funeral.* AMY *enters and comes up behind him.)*

AMY: There's a party?

DANNY: Reception. At my mother's house.

AMY: Somebody, one of your cousins I think, told me there's an ungodly amount of 'the best food you ever ate in your life, sweetheart.'

DANNY: Always is.

AMY: We New England WASPs go for the catered lunch—bland, pathetically skimpy, but with enough booze to mask any unseemly emotions.

DANNY: Might be the best way.

AMY: Pretty sure it's not. *(She sits next to him.)* I'm sorry again. Sounds like he was a great guy.

DANNY: Had a good heart. No irony intended.

AMY: None taken.

DANNY: Little beaten down by life, but…he deserved more.

AMY: More?

DANNY: More time. More…just more.

AMY: Don't we all.

DANNY: That's debatable.

(AMY *takes out a flask, drinks, and hands it to* DANNY. *During this,* ROBERT *enters in tie and overcoat.)*

ROBERT: Hey, I was lookin' for you guys. Your mother asked us to pick up a case of wine. Oh, and more Italian bread.

(DANNY *stares at the flask. Drinks)*

DANNY: Okay.

ROBERT: His father used to make the best Italian
sandwiches. Olive oil, no mayo. Guess Danny's gonna
have to take over the sandwich making duties from
now on, huh? *(No answer.)* Then the pastries they
have…cannolis. Best thing you ever tasted. *(To* AMY*)*
You're staying, aren't you?

AMY: I have an audition this afternoon. Improv troupe
that maybe I want to be part of and maybe I don't.

ROBERT: Hey, that's cool though.

AMY: We'll see. *(Points off stage)* Your Uncle Somebody
is giving me a ride to the train station.

(AMY *waves offstage.* DANNY *looks at the uncle.)*

DANNY: Careful he doesn't make any stops along the
way.

AMY: I know all about dealing with uncles—the good,
the bad and the ugly.

DANNY: If you say so.

AMY: When will you be back?

DANNY: Late tonight.

AMY: You have my number, right? *(Lightly punches him
on the arm)* Right?

DANNY: Yeah, right, I do.

AMY: Then use it sometime, will you. *(No answer)* Okay
then. *(She stands.)* See you, Robby, Robert. Bob.

ROBERT: See you, Amy.

(AMY *walks off toward Uncle Somebody.)*

ROBERT: Wanna go?

DANNY: Not yet.

(ROBERT *sits next to* DANNY.*))*

ROBERT: Nice of Amy to show up, huh?

DANNY: Yeah.

ROBERT: I like her.

DANNY: He was eighty when he died. 1992.

ROBERT: Your father?

DANNY: I'm sure I remember this. We had a party for him. He died a few months later.

ROBERT: Geez.

DANNY: In my other life I would go home every Christmas, stay through New Year's.

ROBERT: I remember you did that last year.

DANNY: And if there was snow to shovel…

ROBERT: *(Understanding)* Oh. Oh, I see what you're saying.

DANNY: I'm responsible.

ROBERT: You mean for…?

DANNY: For my father's death, yes, I'm responsible.

ROBERT: No…how could you be? How could you know? You're not, Danny.

DANNY: *(Not buying it)* I'm making all these choices, changing schools, the apartment…all these things to make my life turn out better, solve problems that I had and…all I'm doing is making everything so much worse.

ROBERT: Wish Uncle Edgar was around.

DANNY: There's something else, too.

ROBERT: What?

DANNY: I'm losing my memory. My *future* memory. I was thinking, for instance, I'd bet the Super Bowl this

year. Steelers or Vikings. I'm a sports guy I should
know that result, right? Nothing. No recollection.
Presidential election…Carter next year, I'm almost
sure, then…Mondale? Maybe. But after that…? Last
night I started a list of all the things that I remember
are going to happen. I'm writing this whole list out
but, honestly, I didn't know. All the stuff I think I
remember may just be wishful thinking, or dreams, or
nothing at all.

ROBERT: Back to life as we know it.

DANNY: Only worse.

ROBERT: You know I been reading these J. W. Dunne
books – they're really complicated, but I'm pretty sure
there's another idea that I kinda understand.

DANNY: *(Reluctantly)* What is it?

ROBERT: You're an observer, you know, from *time 2*?
(DANNY *sighs.)* And you stepped back into your own
life. Like we talked about before, you chose a time and
stepped back in.

DANNY: *(Getting impatient)* Okay, fine, I stepped back
in.

ROBERT: But then sometimes…well, this is what J W
Dunne theorizes…the observer who does that, *you*,
might decide he wants to make changes in his old life.
Then because you're making different choices along
the way, you begin to get lost in your new life. Lost in
time. So eventually, like you were saying, you don't
even remember the old future. You just have a whole
new life with completely different results.

(DANNY *is just staring at him.)*

ROBERT: What do you think?

DANNY: You're saying, I was observing my life,
decided to step back in, then went ahead and made

choices that destroy my relationship with Gwen, kill
off my father, and cause, God knows, what other
catastrophic events? I think it's all *bullshit*, that's what
I think. And how did I even get to *time 2* in the first
place? Does J W Dunne have an answer for that?

ROBERT: Oh...well, yeah, as a matter of fact...that's
the other thing I learned in my reading. See, there are
only two known ways to get to these other levels—you
either access them in your dreams, and we already
figured that you're not dreaming, or...

DANNY: Or...?

ROBERT: Or, you know, after you die.

(DANNY *stares at* ROBERT.)

ROBERT: So, that morning you woke up in our
apartment, maybe the night before in San Francisco...
something happened.

(DANNY *sits with this for a moment. He then starts to
laugh.*)

DANNY: Oh, that's great. Now on top of it all, I have a
death sentence hanging over me.

ROBERT: I mean you could try exercising more.

DANNY: You know what, Robert...it doesn't even
matter when I die. Because right now I need to get
Gwen back. Because that is the *one thing* I am sure
about. And if all this theorizing doesn't help me do
that, then fuck it.

ROBERT: Well, maybe...

DANNY: Maybe what?

ROBERT: Maybe that's why you came back when you
did. You're not supposed to get her back. You have
other plans for yourself.

DANNY: Are you out of your *fucking* mind! There are no other plans.

ROBERT: Except…

DANNY: Except *what?*

ROBERT: Us.

DANNY: Us…what are you talking about?

ROBERT: You said yourself that we stay friends. That we go to San Francisco together, our kids play together…

DANNY: You're the one who said that.

ROBERT: Yeah, but you said it was true. And here we are, staying friends. Probably closer than ever, right? So maybe we go to San Francisco ourselves, you know, and I marry Scarlett Johansen, like you told me—

DANNY: *(Really frustrated now)* Jesus, Robert, I made all that shit up. I don't know the name of the woman you marry, or even if you marry.

ROBERT: But still we stay friends in San Francisco.

DANNY: No, I'm sorry, none of that is going to happen. I go to San Francisco. I'm a journalist. You're an accountant. You go back to Wisconsin to work for your father.

ROBERT: I don't want to do that though.

DANNY: Nevertheless, you do.

ROBERT: Then…what? Do we visit each other?

DANNY: Jesus.

ROBERT: I mean we stay in touch, right?

DANNY: No, we don't. After school, we go our own ways—that much I'm sure about.

ROBERT: That can't be right.

DANNY: It is.

ROBERT: *(Getting desperate)* You told me before, just a minute ago, you're forgetting things.

DANNY: I remember this.

ROBERT: Well, then fuck it, we can change all that. Because you've stepped back into your life you can change things to the way you want them to be. Like in our case—

(DANNY takes him by the shoulders.)

DANNY: *(Trying to be gentle)* Listen to me. You go back to Wisconsin to work for your father. I'm sure you meet someone to marry, have kids, raise a swell family, live a happy, fulfilling life. I just have nothing more to do with it.

ROBERT: But this is what I'm telling you, you can change these things now—

DANNY: *(Putting an end to this)* And I'm telling you, I'm not changing another *fucking* thing! *(Beat)* I'm sorry, Robert. We don't stay friends.

(Long pause)

ROBERT: You know…before all this happened…you were a much nicer guy. *(He walks off.)*

Scene 3

(DANNY takes off his coat and tie. We are back in his East Village apartment, two months later. He gets out two Chinese food to-go containers and chopsticks. Amy comes in through the front door.)

AMY: Chinese food on Saint Paddy's Day?

DANNY: Family tradition.

AMY: Fucking weirdoes. Got forks?

DANNY: The kitchen.

(AMY *goes off to the kitchen. During this* DANNY *also gets a bottle of vodka and two glasses. He pours a decent amount of the vodka in both glasses, then sips at his.*)

AMY: (*Offstage*) Never been coordinated enough to use chopsticks.

DANNY: Takes practice is all.

(AMY *reenters with a fork. Sees the vodka.*)

AMY: This for me?

DANNY: Who else?

AMY: (*Picking up her glass*) Not worried about spoiling shit anymore?

DANNY: Not anymore. Slainte.

AMY: Slainte agad-sa! How does a good Italian boy know Gaelic?

DANNY: Many, many taverns.

(AMY *and* DANNY *drink. He drains his glass. Pours himself another larger shot*)

AMY: Good thing you called when you did.

DANNY: Why is that?

AMY: Tomorrow morning, I am off to the wild blue yonder.

DANNY: Oh yeah?

AMY: Yeah. Believe it or not, little old me has been accepted into a *very* elite San Franciscan improv troupe. Oh yes, every Friday night and twice on Saturdays, 'Zeitgeist' plays sold-out houses for upwards of twenty-five humanoids. (AMY *takes a large bite of the food.*) Mm, fucking delicious.

(DANNY *seems to remember something.*)

DANNY: San Francisco.

AMY: Ten bucks a show I get paid. My big break. Aren't you going to congratulate me?

DANNY: Sure it's the right choice for you?

AMY: Why, will you miss me?

DANNY: It's a long way, you're an East Coast girl, all your friends are here, your sister…

AMY: Not for long, my sister.

DANNY: Oh yeah, right.

AMY: I'm not dropping off the face of the earth. I'll be back for the wedding, of course.

DANNY: *(Trying for nonchalance)* Of course.

AMY: Preparations are heavily under way.

(DANNY *seems deep in thought.*)

AMY: Any queries on the matter? Come on, I'm sure you're dying to know *everything.*

DANNY: What is there to know.

AMY: Let's see, how about, "Is the lovely maiden having second thoughts?"

DANNY: Is she?

AMY: There we go. You pretend to be so disinterested— "Come on over, Amy, we'll get some Chinese food." Hah! When really all you want is to rescue the lovely Gwen from evil prince Chip. Am I right, or am I right?

DANNY: I've written to her. Every week practically—

AMY: You're wasting your time.

DANNY: You could arrange a meeting.

AMY: Fuck that.

DANNY: What do you care anyway, you're off to San Francisco.

AMY: No, I'm not "fucking that" because I want you for myself. I gave up on that idea months ago. I'm 'fucking that' because she's not interested in you anymore. Or she's convinced herself she's not, which turns out to be the same difference. She's sick of people telling her what to do. Kinda leaves you and me out in the cold, doesn't it?

DANNY: Tell her we're having a thing.

AMY: A *thing*?

DANNY: That we're dating.

AMY: Ha-ha.

DANNY: She's concerned about you. Concerned I'm taking advantage. If she knows we're seeing each other then she'll most likely come here. I can at least talk to her again.

AMY: Sorry, pal, no more participation in your bullshit.

(Pause. AMY eats. DANNY stares at her.)

DANNY: We'll make a deal then.

AMY: What kind of deal?

DANNY: I can help you with something. And if I do that, you help me see Gwen.

AMY: What the fuck could you possibly help me with?

(DANNY goes to his desk and takes out a small journal.)

DANNY: These "visions" that I've had, like the fight… I'm not having them anymore. A while ago I wrote down all the future events that I was sure I knew…

AMY: I don't want to know my future if that's where this is headed

DANNY: *(Pressing on)* These people you're working with in San Francisco—

AMY: I told you, I don't want to know.

DANNY: *(Insistent)* No, you need to listen. There're a lot of drugs apparently, and—

AMY: Christ, what a dickbrain you are! She's in Darien tonight, all right? Now fuck off!

DANNY: Darien?

AMY: Wedding bullshit—tasting cakes—decided to spend the night. Chip's not with her, and Mom and Dad are away for the weekend. So there, your big chance. Live long and prosper.

DANNY: You mean…?

AMY: *(Spelling it out)* Gwen is alone in our house in Darien right fucking now as we are speaking, dolt.

DANNY: That's…that's great. Thank you for telling me. *(He looks towards the door.)*

AMY: I'll clean up. Don't worry, I won't steal anything.

(AMY gathers up the containers. DANNY is not moving.)

DANNY: Sure.

AMY: Fucking go already!

(AMY brusquely takes everything to the kitchen. DANNY looks at his journal.)

DANNY: *(Calls out to her)* Promise me something first before I leave.

AMY: I never make promises.

DANNY: Cancel your trip. Tomorrow to San Francisco. Cancel it.

(AMY returns.)

AMY: Why? Cause a bunch of improv comedians take drugs. Oooh, how unusual. What ever will I do amidst all that debauchery? Fucking join the real world will you.

DANNY: *(Refers to his journal)* It's more than that. I don't remember everything exactly—

AMY: Then why are you opening your big mouth?

DANNY: Because things don't go well for you.

AMY: Like that never happens.

DANNY: And this drug habit somewhere along the way—

AMY: Christ! You know what, Petrelli, I've heard enough.

DANNY: It gets worse though...

AMY: *Fuck you, I said I heard enough.*

(AMY starts towards the door. DANNY grabs her, and harshly turns her around.)

AMY: Hey.

DANNY: You overdose.

AMY: You are a fucking psychotic liar. That doesn't happen.

DANNY: Your new apartment, the apartment you have out there, the address... *(He quickly finds a page in the journal.)* It's on Fillmore Street, right? A laundry next door, a little Italian restaurant across the street?

AMY: How the fuck would you know that?

DANNY: Because that's my building, too. Or will be. Or was. And that's where I met Gwen, the first time, because after your memorial service she stayed on a few days to clean out your place. She never married Chip; she was living in New York. We met because you died.

(AMY is trembling.)

DANNY: It's not just visions of the future I had, Amy. I lived this whole other life. And I came back. I don't

even know how, but I came back. Except…you see
it's all different now. Most of it. And your part can be
different, too. Take the notebook. There's other stuff in
here you might find useful. Just cancel your trip, okay.

(A long moment passes. Then AMY *grabs the vodka bottle
and starts to walk around the room.)*

AMY: You know, it's amazing, Danny…it is amazing
how I always, always end up in the same miserable
place. Why is that do you suppose? You who knows
all.

DANNY: Hard to be happy.

AMY: Hard's okay. *Impossible,* that's the real fucking
problem.

DANNY: Yeah, well…you have a lot going for you so—

AMY: *(Turning on him)* No. Pal. You don't know what
I have "going for me". You don't know what it's like
to feel awful about yourself practically every minute
of practically every day. And then when this one thing
comes up, this San Francisco thing, where even though
I'm only earning thirty stinking dollars a week, I still
feel like maybe I did some fucking good job there in
getting that job, that maybe I'm actually turning my
life around, well, when you inform me this 'good job'
will turn out to be the worst thing I ever do, then hell…
kind of bums a girl out.

DANNY: There are other jobs, other groups—

AMY: But why go through all the misery, genius? If I'm
a goner anyway, why even fucking try? *(Suddenly she
smashes the bottle against the wall. The bottle breaks so she's
holding only a jagged edge.)*

DANNY: Hey! What the hell… Are you crazy?

AMY: Well, yes sir, as a matter of fact, I am.

DANNY: Look I told you this to warn you. You can correct the course you're on. Fight for your life, make things better for yourself—

AMY: Is that what you've done? Since you lived your life already and now have your "second chance". Have you corrected the mistakes? Or just turned yourself into a more miserable bastard than you were to begin with? Because that's sure as hell what it looks like to me.

(AMY *starts to dig the broken glass into one of her wrists.* DANNY *rushes at her and grabs the hand with the broken glass.*)

DANNY: Hey, what the hell!

(AMY *and* DANNY *struggle. She swings the jagged glass at him, barely missing him.*)

AMY: Get the fuck back.

DANNY: (*Stumbling backwards*) Jesus.

AMY: Fuck you! Fuck you, Petrelli. Fuck you...

(AMY *is weeping now. Her wrist is bleeding. She drops the bottle.* DANNY *grabs a dish towel.*)

DANNY: Here, you're bleeding. Hold this on your wrist. Christ, Amy, we...we should get you to the hospital.

AMY: I don't need the fucking hospital.

(DANNY *has the towel secured around her wrist.* AMY *slowly collapses onto the floor. He is holding her.*)

DANNY: I just want to make sure you're not hurt that's all.

AMY: I'm not hurt. It's nothing. I'm nothing so why the fuck should you care.

DANNY: I'll call someone—your mother or father, Gwen—?

AMY: No. Fucking no. I don't need anyone. Don't fucking call anyone.

DANNY: All right. All right. I won't call. Just…take a breath.

AMY: *(Through tears)* You said you couldn't help.

DANNY: What?

AMY: In Vegas, you said, "I can't help you, Amy".

DANNY: *(Affected by this)* I didn't know. I'm sorry. I'm really sorry.

AMY: Fuck, I feel sick.

DANNY: That's okay. Come on, I'll take you to the bathroom. We'll get this cut cleaned up, too. Come on.

(DANNY helps AMY up, she is still crying.)

AMY: Oh god, what a disaster I am.

DANNY: You're not. Don't worry…you're just screwed up like everyone else.

AMY: *(Quietly)* Gwen is alone in Darien. You'll miss your chance…

DANNY: All right, I'll miss it. I'm not going anywhere. I'm staying with you. I'll help you. I can help you. Come on…

(DANNY and AMY slowly walk to the bathroom. Lights change.)

Scene 4

(A beautiful late morning, Memorial Day weekend in Darien, Connecticut. There is a long moment of silence. ROBERT enters, looking quite sheepish. He is holding a small knapsack and a very large box of chocolates. He walks downstage and stands by the porch furniture. We are in the WEST's family house. After several moments, AMY walks in. She's wearing pajamas.)

AMY: *(Delighted to see ROBERT)* Look who's here.

ROBERT: Hey, yeah.

AMY: You're such a sweet guy. How did you ever get to be so sweet?

(AMY and ROBERT hug and will eventually sit.)

ROBERT: Comes natural, I guess. I brought you chocolates. I didn't know if…you know if it was something you'd want.

AMY: Didn't know? What else could I want? What else could I possibly be dreaming about?

ROBERT: Would you like me to…?

AMY: Yeah, come on, open that baby up.

(ROBERT goes to work on opening the chocolates.)

AMY: My mother keeps bringing me plates of vegetables with dip. Because apparently if we only eat enough raw broccoli smothered in ranch dressing all will be right in the world.

ROBERT: I hate vegetables. Give me a burger any day.

AMY: You said it, brother.

(ROBERT has the box open.)

AMY: Hmmm, look at these beauties.

ROBERT: Damn, they got whites in there.

AMY: *(Examining the chocolates)* Oh yeah. No one likes that bullshit, do they? Who invented that white chocolate bullshit anyway?

ROBERT: A crazy man. Wanna…?

(AMY starts picking out chocolates.)

AMY: You kidding? I'm taking one of these, and one of these, aaaand this little piggy.

(AMY starts to consume her three chocolates. ROBERT takes one of the white ones and nibbles at it.)

AMY: Hey, what are you doing? Don't eat that.

ROBERT: No really, it's not so bad. I wanna leave the good ones for you.

AMY: Aw. You *are* such a sweet guy. In every possible way.

ROBERT: My mother likes me.

AMY: I bet she does.

(GWEN appears.)

GWEN: Robert. I heard you were here.

ROBERT: Yeah, I showed up.

GWEN: You are so sweet. Isn't he sweet?

AMY: I told him already. And look what he brought.

GWEN: Oh, come on. I have a wedding dress to fit into.

(GWEN sits next to AMY and starts to search through the chocolate box.)

AMY: He brought them for me, not you.

GWEN: I don't care, I'm under a lot of stress. Why do they always put in so many whites?

AMY: I know, right?

GWEN: Can't be any cheaper to make, plus nobody likes them. *(She puts a whole chocolate in her mouth.)*

ROBERT: They're really not too bad.

GWEN: *(Relishing the taste)* Oh, Jesus, Mary and Joseph, these are so fucking good.

AMY: Robert is our savoir. He has come here today to save us from our afternoon vegetable platter.

ROBERT: Maybe I should get another box.

GWEN: Yes, do that, Robert. That would be so wonderful. Go right now and get, oh, I don't know, *ten* boxes, to get us through the week.

AMY: No, he can't leave. He's my friend, I want him here.

GWEN: He's my friend, too.

ROBERT: I'm everybody's friend. More chocolates!

(They eat happily in silence for a few moments.)

ROBERT: So, Amy, how you doin' anyway?

(AMY finishes a chocolate. GWEN watches her.)

AMY: Me? Oh, Robby, I am having the time of my life. My sister can bear witness. Let's see, there's T V, staring into space, two therapy sessions a week, plus group on Saturdays, more staring into space, keeping track of my pills…sitting on the toilet till my legs go numb, more staring…

GWEN: She's doing better. Figuring a lot of things out, aren't you?

AMY: Yeah, that's me. Contemplator of life.

ROBERT: Get lots of visitors?

GWEN: Our mother's friends mostly.

AMY: Patty. Patty's here, Amy. Doesn't Patty have anything else to do?

GWEN: She's nice, though. Her husband left her, they never had kids…

AMY: Fancies herself a Good Samaritan. Yuck!

GWEN: *She's nice.*

AMY: Yes, but why must she take it out on me.

ROBERT: How about *your* friends?

AMY: What friends?

GWEN: She asked them to stay away for now.

AMY: Too awkward. That's why I'm never letting you leave, Robby. You will be living in my room with me from now on.

ROBERT: I'm happy to stay.

GWEN: You done with school?

ROBERT: Graduated Friday.

GWEN: Me, too.

AMY: And…?

ROBERT: Out of money. My father wants me to go home. Work with him this summer. Trying to avoid that if I can.

AMY: Watch out, or you'll end up like Jimmy Stewart in that movie.

ROBERT: Oh yeah, I know the one you mean. I always feel so bad he never gets to go on his trips.

AMY: And all those retarded kids to deal with. I tell you, it's a fucking tragedy.

GWEN: The movie's called, *It's a Wonderful Life,* no irony intended.

AMY: Mm-hm. Good luck with that.

(Beat)

AMY: *(Asking casually)* Ever see Danny?

(AMY looks over at GWEN, who looks away.)

ROBERT: No. Not since his father's funeral.

AMY: Hasn't shown up here either.

GWEN: Better for all involved, don't you think?

ROBERT: He did send me something though. For my graduation.

AMY: A gift?

ROBERT: Kinda. Pretty unusual actually. One of the reasons I wanted to come, besides seeing you guys, of course.

AMY: We're on pins and needles, aren't we, Gwen?

GWEN: *(Neutral)* What did he send you?

ROBERT: Uh…a little notebook. Like a journal. Don't quite know what to make of it.

(ROBERT *reaches into his knapsack and pulls out the journal* DANNY *had tried to give to* AMY *in the previous scene. She seems to tense up.*)

ROBERT: *(Reads from the cover page)* "Congratulations. This may do you some future good."

GWEN: What's in there?

AMY: You don't want to know. Nobody wants to know. Throw the thing away.

ROBERT: I already read it, though.

AMY: All the way through?

ROBERT: Yeah, three or four times.

GWEN: What does it say?

ROBERT: That's the mystery.

AMY: He wrote down everything he thinks he knows about the future, that's what's in there.

GWEN: And showed it to you?

AMY: Tried to.

GWEN: Oh god.

ROBERT: But this is the thing, most of what's written here...he crossed it out. Can't even read anything really, except for a few...well, couple of things that are circled... *(He is leafing through the book.)* Like here, "Red Sox win World Series. Year, question mark." What good does that do me?

(AMY takes the journal, and starts to skim through, reading an occasional bit.)

AMY: Son of a bitch... "E T phone home." The fuck is that?

ROBERT: Weird.

AMY: *(Flipping pages)* "Osama/Obama." It rhymes anyway. "Apple." Mean anything to you?

ROBERT: A lotta weird shit.

AMY: I swear the guy is certifiable.

ROBERT: There's a drawing in the back. Pretty good, too. Didn't know he had artistic talent.

(AMY goes to the back page. Stares at the drawing)

GWEN: What's it of?

AMY: Two little kids.

(AMY puts the book down on the table so GWEN can see it. GWEN looks at the drawing. She cannot look away.)

ROBERT: Weird, huh?

AMY: I'd forget about it if I were you. Hey, it's hot back here, how about a root beer float? You like root beer floats?

ROBERT: I love root beer floats.

AMY: Good, let's get you one. Gwenny?

GWEN: *(Not taking her eyes off the drawing)* No, I...have stuff to do.

AMY: Suit yourself. Come on, Robby.

(As AMY *stands, she watches* GWEN *for a long moment. Then, arm-in-arm, she and* ROBERT *walk off to the kitchen. After they are gone,* GWEN *carefully rips the drawing out of the notebook, folds it and puts it into her pocket. She then closes the book and places it back in* ROBERT's *knapsack. She stands and slowly walks into the main room.)*

Scene 5

(We are back in DANNY's *apartment. A week later.* GWEN *waits, quietly, in the middle of the room. He enters the apartment. He is carrying a few empty cardboard boxes. He stops. Very surprised to see* GWEN*)*

DANNY: Gwen…?

GWEN: Hi.

DANNY: I…I didn't…you're the last person I expected—

GWEN: The door was open.

*(*DANNY *puts the boxes down.)*

DANNY: Yeah, had to run out for a second.

GWEN: Going somewhere?

DANNY: I'm moving. Tomorrow, as a matter of fact.

GWEN: Out of the city?

DANNY: Brooklyn. Got behind in school, have to go back for another semester. Thought it best to conserve my money for a while.

GWEN: You'll miss being in the village.

DANNY: I will.

GWEN: I think I'm supposed to be hitting you with a baseball bat right about now.

DANNY: Too late. *(Beat. Her watches her.)* Aren't you getting married?

GWEN: Tomorrow morning. Tonight's the rehearsal dinner.

DANNY: Ah. *(He checks his watch.)* After three. No *preparations?* Wedding day whatevers?

GWEN: My mother is maniacally well organized. I'm going with the flow. All you can do, really.

DANNY: Okay, but still…?

GWEN: I told her I needed to go into the city because my trousseau is incomplete.

DANNY: You really used that word, trousseau?

GWEN: I did. Worked like a charm. *(Beat)* I wasn't sure whether to stop by here or not. Whether I wanted to. Walked around the block several times after I arrived. Part of me was hoping you'd be gone off somewhere.

DANNY: I'm here.

GWEN: Yes, I see.

(Another beat. DANNY really doesn't know what to make of this.)

GWEN: Robert is going to be living with us, by the way.

DANNY: Living with who?

GWEN: At my parents' house, in their basement apartment. My father got him a job. They'll be commuting into the city together, I guess.

DANNY: Wow…that was nice of him.

GWEN: He likes to take in strays. And Robert seems to be awfully good company for Amy, so…

DANNY: I see. How is Amy?

GWEN: Much better. Probably better than she's been in years, we hope.

DANNY: Good.

GWEN: My family is grateful to you. I'm grateful. How you took care of her that night, stayed with her till the morning. That meant a lot.

DANNY: If I was in any way responsible—

GWEN: You weren't. She hadn't been taking her medication. It was a long time coming. I'm glad you were there. *(A beat)* Anyway, that's the real reason why I came, to thank you.

(DANNY nods. GWEN looks at her watch.)

GWEN: There's a four-ten train, should probably catch it. Union Station the closest subway?

DANNY: *(Gets his wallet out)* Take a cab. Traffic's bad however you go but might as well be comfortable. *(Holds out a ten-dollar bill)*

GWEN: Don't be silly, I have money.

DANNY: My treat. Please…it'll give me pleasure to buy you a cab ride.

GWEN: *(Takes the money)* Awfully nice.

(Neither DANNY nor GWEN move for a moment.)

GWEN: I had one of Robert's dreams the other night.

DANNY: *Robert's* dreams?

GWEN: His prescient dreams that he talked about.

DANNY: Uh-huh.

GWEN: I was on a train, leaving my house, my parent's house…all of a sudden, I got so scared because the train wasn't stopping, just taking me further and further away. I had no idea where I was or where I was going, and I had no way of getting off. Finally, I started to bang on the windows, like a crazy woman, yell at the other passengers…they could all care less; even when a conductor finally came through and I tried

explaining how much I needed to get off this stupid
train, he just walked right by. When I woke up, I was
shaking…weeping. Then today, on the train coming
here…I felt the exact same thing…like I was desperate
to get off at the next stop, take the next train home,
but the train I was on was an express, so we just kept
whizzing by all these other stations. I was praying
we'd stop, somewhere. I felt that same panic, that same
desperation I felt in my dream. That same awful feeling
of being hopelessly lost.

DANNY: But you got off at Grand Central.

GWEN: I did. *(Beat)* Danny…?

DANNY: Yes.

GWEN: Do you still believe? In everything you said to
me…that we had a life together. Do you still believe
that?

DANNY: I do. I can't explain it. I'll never be able to
explain it. And most of it is a jumble in my mind now,
so really it doesn't even matter anymore—whether it
was real, or a dream, or fantasy, or whatever – but…
yes, I'll always believe. That won't ever change.

(GWEN nods; starts to exit, until…)

DANNY: I want you to know…that in our life
together…I wasn't a good husband. Not at all what
you deserved. I drank too much, too often, was
obsessed with work…when you wanted to move back
to New York, you wanted that so badly, I ignored you.
And then… *(Hard to get this out.)*

GWEN: You don't have to—

DANNY: I do, I'm sorry. I had an affair…with this
woman, a co-worker. It had gone on for a long time,
you found out… That last night before I woke up in
Boston, we weren't together, because you were gone. I
let you go. I screwed up our life, you see? I didn't love

you the way you deserved to be loved. And if I could do it all over again…if I could, I wouldn't let a day go by, not an hour, when I wouldn't show you how much you mean to me, when I wouldn't make something of every moment we have together. Because you deserve that. And I know it doesn't mean anything to you now, but…I'm sorry. I'm sorry I let you down. I'm sorry.

(DANNY *looks away.* GWEN *watches him. She looks around the apartment. Eventually she walks up next to him. From her pocket, she pulls out the drawing of the two children. She holds the drawing out so he can see.*)

GWEN: What are their names?

DANNY: Who?

GWEN: Our children. What are their names?

(*For a long moment,* DANNY *stares at the drawing. Finally, he looks up at* GWEN. *They find each other, as if for the first time. Blackout*)

END OF PLAY

CPSIA information can be obtained
at www.ICGtesting.com
Printed in the USA
JSRC021132100622
26891JS00007B/22